# Prayer Magick Miracles

82 powerful prayers for instant manifestation and connection with the divine.

Embracing the Divine Presence

## SHEETAL SAPAN MHATRE

**BLUEROSE PUBLISHERS**
India | U.K.

Copyright © Sheetal Sapan Mhatre 2023

All rights reserved by author. No part of this publication may be reproduced, stored in a retrieval system or transmitted in any form or by any means, electronic, mechanical, photocopying, recording or otherwise, without the prior permission of the author. Although every precaution has been taken to verify the accuracy of the information contained herein, the publisher assumes no responsibility for any errors or omissions. No liability is assumed for damages that may result from the use of information contained within.

BlueRose Publishers takes no responsibility for any damages, losses, or liabilities that may arise from the use or misuse of the information, products, or services provided in this publication.

For permissions requests or inquiries regarding this publication, please contact:

BLUEROSE PUBLISHERS
www.BlueRoseONE.com
info@bluerosepublishers.com
+91 8882 898 898
+4407342408967

ISBN: 978-93-5819-247-6

Cover design: Muskan Sachdeva
Typesetting: Pooja Sharma

First Edition: December 2023

# Acknowledgement

I know angels are real because I have seen them in the form of my husband Sapan, and my parents Vasant & Vrushali Dhuri. Thank you for your encouragement and support.

I am also grateful to my daughter Shreemi for choosing me as her mother and enriching my life.

I thank God, Goddess and Archangels for everything and for giving these beautiful prayers as a download.

Thank you Heena and my entire team for being a great support.

## Introduction to the Book

What is your first memory of a prayer? and what was it for? Did your prayer get answered? Who empowered you with this tool? All these question popped up when I was wondering how I should start the introduction of this book.

It may sound cliché but I have to say it, this book has found you as the divine wants to create a positive shift in your life. Our future is not written in stone; you can create an amazing future with the help of prayers, mindset and action.

In my tarot and angel consultations, there were times when the cards were not positive and I told the querent not to get disheartened, do the prayers, take required action and change the future. They followed the guidance and experienced major shifts.

This book will do the 50% part by creating the required energy however the other 50% is in your hands in the form of action. I am often asked why to pray if the divine knows everything then why can't it simply give? Well, the divine can give only if you ask due to the law of free will. The part of asking is nothing but prayer. Let me share an example: Lord Krishna was asked why he did not help the Pandavas to which he replied I was waiting for them to ask me for intervention as I cannot go against the law of free will hence when Draupadi called me I immediately intervened.

Some of you must be wondering what the law of free will is. We all, before being born on earth, sit with our guides and decide the lessons that we will learn and how our life story is going to be which is called a blueprint. However, we get excited and take really hard lessons despite our guides convincing us not to take such hard lessons. After being born on earth we find the lessons too tough and feel helpless, and due to the law of free will the divine can't intervene unless and until we ask for help.

Asking for help is nothing but saying prayers. This powerful tool can modify or change this blueprint or help us to learn the lessons in an easier manner.

I observed that many people needed a structured word format that did justice to their request. I hence started sharing prayers on my Facebook page Spiritual Retreat by Sheetal Sapan Mhatre and it created a shift in many people's lives, subscribers had to scroll a lot to find prayers so I thought let me share it in a book so it becomes easy to access.

I hope and pray that these prayers create miracles in

your life. Do refer to the frequently answered questions for more clarity.

# Contents

### A. Prayers for Beauty

| | |
|---|---|
| 01. Prayer for Beautiful Hair | 1 |
| 02. Prayer for Beautiful Skin | 2 |
| 03. Prayer for Beauty | 3 |
| 04. Prayer for Mind, Body & Soul | 4 |

### B. Prayers for Health, Fitness & Safety

| | |
|---|---|
| 05. Prayer for Women's Gynae Health | 5 |
| 06. Prayer for Good Health | 6 |
| 07. Prayer for Healing Depression & Other Emotional Issues | 8 |
| 08. Prayer to Heal Body Pain | 9 |
| 09. Prayer for Raising food vibrations | 10 |
| 10. Prayer for good sleep & avoiding nightmares | 11 |
| 11. Prayer for Ideal Body Weight | 12 |
| 12. Prayer for Healing Covid Positive Patient | 14 |
| 13. Prayer for Emotional Wisdom | 16 |
| 14. Prayer for Hospitalized Patient | 17 |

15. Prayer for Peace and Positivity   18
16. Prayer to Release resistance   19
17. Prayer for Forgiveness   20
18. Healing prayer for Eyes   21
19. Healing prayer for Thyroid   22
20. Healing prayer for Teeth   23

### C. Prayers For Protection
21. Protection Prayer While Driving   24
22. Prayer for Cleansing Energy in Shower   25
23. Prayer for Protection   26
24. Prayers for Everyday Protection   27

### D. Prayers For Prosperity & Career
25. Prosperity Prayer for Attracting More Customers & business success   28
26. Prayer to Pay off loan   29
27. Archangel Prayer for Prosperity   30
28. Prayer for Removing Obstacles from Prosperity   32
29. Powerful Prayer for Financial Blessings   33
30. Prayer for Money on Urgent Basis   34
31. Prayer for selling a property or any object   35
32. Prayer for Prosperity consciousness Clearance   36
33. Prayer for Job Interview   37
34. Prayer for Finding Job   38

## E. Prayers For Self

| | |
|---|---|
| 35. Prayer for Self - Acceptance | 39 |
| 36. Prayer for Self-Confidence | 40 |
| 37. Prayer to Stop People from Spoiling Reputation | 41 |
| 38. Prayer for Joy | 42 |
| 39. Prayers for Time Management | 43 |
| 40. Prayer for Life Purpose | 44 |

## F. Prayers For Divine

| | |
|---|---|
| 41. Prayer for Divine Grace during Tough Times | 45 |
| 42. Prayer for Increasing Faith in Divine | 46 |
| 43. Prayer to 9 Forms of Goddess Durga | 47 |
| 44. Prayer to Seek Miracles | 49 |
| 45. Prayer to Show God's Presence | 50 |

## G. Prayers For Pregnancy & Children

| | |
|---|---|
| 46. Prayer for Conception | 51 |
| 47. Prayer for Safe Pregnancy | 53 |
| 48. Prayer for Easy Delivery of Child | 54 |

## H. Prayers For Removing Obstacles & Wish Fulfillment

| | |
|---|---|
| 49. Removing Obstacles or Wish Fulfillment Prayer | 55 |
| 50. Lord Ganesha Prayer for Removing Obstacles | 56 |
| 51. Saint Jude Prayer for Wish Fulfilment | 57 |

## I. Harmony in Relationship / Resolving legal cases

| | |
|---|---|
| 52. Prayer for Healing Relationship | 58 |
| 53. Resolution of Conflict Prayer | 59 |

## J. Prayers For Souls

54. Prayer for a Soul Crossing Over — 61
55. Prayers for Ancestral Healing — 62

## K. Prayers For World & Well Being

56. Prayer for World Peace & Well Being — 63
57. Prayer for Country — 65
58. Prayer for Soldier — 66

## L. Academic Success & examination

59. Prayer for Child's Academic Success — 67
60. Prayer for Academic Success — 69

## M. Prayers for Nature

61. Prayer for Adequate Rain and To Stop Excess Rain — 71
62. Prayer If You Are Experiencing Natural Calamity — 72
63. Prayer for Protection from Natural Calamities like Cyclone, Tsunami, Earthquake — 74

## N. Prayer for being a parenting and raising children

64. Prayer for Raising Children — 75
65. Prayer for Safety and Guidance of Children — 76

## O. Prayers for Lost item/person/pet

66. Angel Magick Spell for Finding Lost Item — 78
67. Prayer to Find a Missing Person/Pet — 79

## P. Short Prayers

68. Prayer for Positive Thoughts — 80
69. Prayer for Abundance — 81

| | |
|---|---|
| 70. Prayer during Tough Times | 82 |
| 71. Short Prayers for Hair, Skin and Weight | 83 |
| 72. Prayer for New Year | 84 |
| 73. Short Prayers to Call upon Archangel Chamuel for Love | 85 |

### Q. Other / Generic Prayers

| | |
|---|---|
| 74. Prayer for Everyday | 87 |
| 75. Prayer to Make New Friends | 88 |
| 76. Prayer for Happy Holidays | 89 |
| 77. Prayer for Tarot Readers | 90 |

### R. Prayers For Home

| | |
|---|---|
| 78. Prayer for Cleansing Your Home with Archangel Michael | 91 |
| 79. Prayer for a New Home | 92 |

### S. Prayers For Support

| | |
|---|---|
| 80. Prayer for Finding a Good Maid | 93 |
| 81. Prayer for Finding Employee | 94 |
| 82. Prayer for Decision Making | 95 |

# 01.
# Prayer for Beautiful Hair

Dear God, Goddess, Archangels, it is my will to have gorgeous, long, healthy hair.

I am releasing all blockages that are stopping me from experiencing the pleasure of having long, beautiful hair to divine light.

Please heal each and every cell in my scalp and hair. Please strengthen and nourish my scalp, hair roots, each and every hair strand with your divine light.

Please let my scalp grow hair naturally and beautifully in such a way that I have thick, long, silky, healthy hair.

I thank you from the bottom of my heart for blessing me with beautiful hair, this or better. Thank you.

# 02.
# Prayer for Beautiful Skin

Dear Beauty Gods, Goddess, Archangels it is my will to have beautiful, young, glowing healthy skin. Please bless me with the same.

I release all kinds of blockages to the divine. I call upon Archangel Michael to cleanse each and every pore of my skin & protect it with sacred light.

Archangel Raphael please heal each and every cell of my skin with your celestial emerald green light.

Archangel Jophiel please beautify each & every cell of my skin, blessing it with angelic grace & beauty.

Angels of beauty and youth infuse divine healing energies in my skin in such a way that my skin looks extremely young, healthy & beautiful.

Let the light of the divine shine on my mind, body & soul.

This or better. Thank You.

# 03.
# Prayer for Beauty

Dear Goddess Laxmi, Goddess Aphrodite (Afro-die-tee) and Archangel Jophiel it is my will to be beautiful & gorgeous from head to toe.

Please help me to see beauty in me and appreciate it.

I am excited to be a reflection of your beauty & charm, so bless me with this precious gift now & forever.

This or better. Thank you.

**Note-:** Goddess Laxmi is the goddess of fortune and beauty. Goddess Aphrodite is the goddess of love and beauty.

# 04.
# Prayer for Mind, Body & Soul

Dear God Goddess and Archangels, I am your child. I seek your blessings. I request you to clear all the blockages from mind, body and soul, so that it becomes healthy and beautiful.

Please heal my mind, body and soul, so that I can connect with you easily and effortlessly.

Please illuminate my mind, body and soul with your divine grace and light. Please bless me, so that I experience beauty, enlightenment, healing in each and every cell of my being now and forever. This or better, thank you.

# 05.
# Prayer for Women's Gynae Health

Dear God, Goddess, Archangel Raphael and Archangel Haniel you have blessed me with the gift of being a female.

I accept this gift wholeheartedly and with gratitude.

I request you to balance my hormones perfectly and help me to accept both my feminine and masculine side with grace.

Please send continuous healing energy to my endocrine glands, ovaries, fallopian tube and uterus.

Please heal my body, mind and reproductive organs with your divine light.

Please envelope me in your divine healing shield so that I am healthy and safe in all directions of time.

**Note-:** Archangel Raphael is the angel of healing. Archangel Haniel helps in balancing masculine and feminine aspects.

# 06.
# Prayer for Good Health

Dear God, Goddess, Archangels I really need a lot of courage, emotional and physical strength right now, so please be with me as my guiding light & heal me.

Please send millions and trillions of healing angels to heal each & every cell of my body. please let each cell be washed with divine white light so that they become healthy & I become healthy & fit.

I request you to heal all issues so that my emotional & physical health is excellent now & forever. Please heal my DNA, chakras, organs, emotions, my mind, body and soul.

Please guide me to the right doctor, food, beverages & lifestyle that will heal me completely. please give me the willpower to follow the same.

Please replace every curse with blessing, every stress with peace, every negativity with divine positivity. This or better, Thank you.

**Note-:** This prayer should be said in all kinds of illnesses or for good health once a day, however not meant to replace doctor's advice or treatment. You can do it for family members as well by taking their name.

# 07.
# Prayer for Healing Depression & Other Emotional Issues

Dear God, Goddess and Archangels, please heal each and every cell of my nervous system and body with your white, golden and pink light.

Please heal my soul in all directions of time.

Please bless me with a restful and peaceful sleep, so that my brain is rejuvenated and refreshed.

Please bless me with positive people and experiences that create happiness and blessings in my life.

Please heal my emotions and bless me with compassion. Please help me to love myself & bless me with emotional peace, excellent mental health, physical fitness, joy and positive mindset. This or better. Thank you.

**Note-:** This prayer is for healing depression & other mental imbalance however NOT meant to replace counseling, medicine, doctor's advice.

# 08.
# Prayer to Heal Body Pain

Dear God, Goddess and Archangels, I am ready to let go of my pain in my ………………… (mention body part) for peace in terms of health.

I seek forgiveness for all the karmas that have resulted in this situation.

I also ask you to please remove any negativity that has resulted in this pain.

I ask you to please heal all the cells, nerves, muscles and each part of my body with your powerful rays.

Please bless me with a healthy, fit, body that will help me to live the gift of life peacefully and happily.

This or better thank you.

# 09.
# Prayer for Raising Food Vibrations

Food is a source of energy and it also absorbs energy of the one who cooks and the surrounding. One cannot control the above factors but one can definitely change or modify the energy of food.

Clean your hands and place a few inches above the food or simply fold your hands and say "Dear God, Goddess and Archangels, thank you for the food on our plate. Please bless the ones who cultivate our food, bless the hands that prepare the food. Please remove all the negativity from this food & bless it with your divine light, so that it nourishes and enriches our mind, body and soul. This or better, thank you."

# 10.
# Prayer for Good Sleep & Avoiding Nightmares

Dear God, Goddess Durga, Archangel Michael and my guardian angels please protect me as I sleep.

Please help me to relax and let go. Help me to sleep peacefully so that my mind, body and soul heals with divine grace.

Please let me have no dreams or beautiful dreams. Please bless me with deep sleep so that I wake up in the morning rejuvenated and refreshed. This or better. Thank you.

Note :- Prayer has to be said before going to bed once.

# 11.
# Prayer for Ideal Body Weight

Dear God, Goddess, Archangels and my Guardian angels I surrender my weight struggles to you. I really am ready to be fit, be my ideal body weight and ideal body proportion now and forever.

Please remove and heal any vows, karmas, negativity, curses, addictions, lifestyles patterns, mental and physical blockages that are resulting in imbalance in my weight in all directions of time.

Please heal and build my metabolism in such a way that my body naturally maintains its ideal body weight and proportion.

Please motivate me to eat healthy, drink healthy beverages, I also request you to help me to exercise regularly and in a healthy manner, easily and happily. Please also help me to be at peace and sleep deeply for 8 hours.

I have complete faith and trust that you will help me to treat my body as a divine temple. Please let my body **release excess fat**, toxins easily and comfortably. This or better, thank you.

**Note-:** For gaining weight you will say the above prayer itself however instead of release excess fat you will say gain healthy weight.

# 12.
# Prayer for Healing Covid Positive Patient

Dear God, Goddess and Archangels, please give emotional & physical strength to the ............... (patient name), family, neighbours, so that they are able to combat the corona virus easily.

Please give them the support that they need to overcome this illness with ease.

Archangel Raphael and Lord Hanuman, please heal each and every cell of the ............... (patient's name) with your powerful healing so that he/she is healthy, devoid of any disease. Please strengthen their immunity.

Please let the recovery of the ............... (patient's name) be rapid and in a comfortable manner. Please make him/her healthy, fit & fine.

Archangel Michael, please protect the family members, neighbors of the ................ (patient's name) & all those with whom they have interacted from corona virus and bless them all with good health in all directions of time. Please sanitize their space and surroundings 24/7 with your divine light.

This or better thank you.

Note-: Take proper medical precautions and treatment along with the above prayer.

# 13.
# Prayer for Emotional Wisdom

Dear God, Goddess, Archangels, my guardian angels please fill my mind & heart with positivity and faith. Help me to be at peace.

Bless me with strength & wisdom to accept & follow God's will. Please guide me to channel my emotions in a matured way so that I and others benefit from my emotional wisdom.

Please help me to be secure & happy in other people's happiness & success.

Please help me to forgive & bless those who have hurt me. Please also help the ones whom I have hurt knowingly or unknowingly to forgive & bless me.

Please guide & help me to focus & follow my life purpose in perfect timing. I request you to fill my heart & mind with wisdom, joy, love, positivity, security & peace. This or better, thank you.

Note: - This prayer can be done in mind, focusing on life purpose and overall emotional wisdom.

# 14.
## Prayer for Hospitalized Patient

Dear God, Goddess and Archangels, ........................ (Patient's name) is in the hospital. Please heal each cell in their body. Please send millions of Angels to heal them. Please guide the doctors to give the right treatment so that ................... (patient name) recovers fully & soon.

Please give them and their family members strength to cope up with this process. Please let there be no negative side effects of the medicine taken by patient on their mind and body. Let the medicines heal them.

Please bless them with the finances required for this medical treatment and hospitalization.

Please bless the patient and family members. Bless the doctors, nurses and the hospital staff for the service they provide. This or better. Thank you.

# 15.
# Prayer for Peace and Positivity

Dear God, Goddess, And Archangels I completely surrender to you.

Please enable me to let go of emotions, thoughts, fears that are not serving me, easily and comfortably.

Please replace every negativity, stress in my mind with positivity, joy and peace.

Please take away all my problems and bless me with divine solutions.

I request you to pour so much of positivity in my mind that I shine in the divine light of serenity.

Please send me situations and people that will brighten my life with joy & laughter. Please heal my mind and soul.

Empower me to live my life happily, peacefully, with serenity and faith.

# 16.
## Prayer To Release Resistance

Dear God, please help me to release all kinds of resistance that are blocking my path to divine light so that I can move ahead with confidence, success and clarity.

This or better, thank you.

# 17.
# Prayer for Forgiveness

Dear God, Goddess, my guardian angels

I need to forgive ................. (name) please help me to easily forgive them so that my mind, heart and soul is full of peace and divine light.

I also request you to let all those people whom I have hurt forgive me easily and soon.

Please grant me emotional strength and wisdom. Bless them and bless us.

# 18.
# Healing prayer for Eyes

Dear God, Goddess, Archangel Raphael, Lord Hanuman, Saint Padre Pio please heal each and every cell of my eyes with your loving divine healing energies.

Please let me see this beautiful world that you have created clearly and with ease.

Please replace my fears with trust. I surrender to you and request you to make my eyes and vision healthy. This or better, thank you.

**Note:-

Archangel Raphael is the angel of healing.

Lord Hanuman is the God of healing and protection.

Saint Padre Pio helps with healing eyes.

The above prayer is not meant to replace doctor's advice or medicines.

# 19.
# Healing prayer for Thyroid

Dear God, Goddess, Archangel Raphael and Archangel Gabriel, please heal my Throat chakra, my mind, body and soul. Please help me to communicate clearly with myself and others. This or better. Thank you.

*Note :-

Archangel Gabriel takes care of throat chakra.

The above prayer is not meant to replace doctor's advice or medicines.*

# 20.
# Healing prayer for Teeth

Archangel Raphael is the Angel of healing. Every day and night while brushing your teeth say,

"Divine Archangel Raphael heal my teeth, gums with your emerald green light & make my teeth and gums healthy, this or better, thank you."

**Note :-

Archangel Raphael is the angel of healing.

The above prayer is not meant to replace doctor's advice or medicines.

# 21.
# Protection Prayer While Driving

Dear God, Goddess, Archangel Michael and my Guardian angels, please be with me and keep me safe when I am driving. Please protect everyone in and around my vehicle and also protect my and other people's vehicles on the road. Let me reach safe and sound to my home or _____ (mention destination). This or better. Thank you.

**Note -:** This prayer should be done before driving the car or vehicle.

This prayer can be said by the one driving the car or the passenger.

Drive safe.

# 22.
# Prayer for Cleansing Energy in Shower

Whenever you are in shower say this

"Dear God, Goddess, Archangel Michael please cleanse my mind, body, soul & each and every cell in my body & envelope me in your purple shield,

this or better, thank you."

# 23.
# Prayer for Protection

Dear God, Goddess, please send Archangel Michael & his band of mercy to cut all the cords, remove all kinds of negativity lower energies, entities from my mind body, my aura, soul & every cell of my being & protect me in your Divine light now and forever.

I also request you to remove from the roots all cords, remove all kinds of negativity, lower energies, entities from my family's mind, body, soul, aura & every cell of their being & protect them in divine light, now and forever.

This or better.

Thank you! Thank you! Thank you!

# 24.
# Prayers for Everyday Protection

Dear God, Goddess & Archangel Michael please envelope me, our home, & my family in your divine shield so that we are safe from all kinds of emotional, physical and spiritual harm in all directions of time.

# 25.
# Prosperity Prayer for Attracting More Customers & Business Success

Dear God, Goddess, Archangel Ariel and Archangel Chamuel I have ………….. business and I offer ………………….. products or ……………….. service, whoever will benefit from my products / services please give them the wisdom, finances and willingness to purchase my ……………………….. products / services so that we both mutually benefit from our professional association, this or better, thank you.

**Note-:** Archangel Ariel is the angel of prosperity

Archangel Chamuel helps in finding anything.

# 26.
## Prayer to Pay Off Loan

Dear God, Goddess Abundantia, Goddess Lakshmi, Lord Narayana, Goddess Green Tara, Goddess Aeracura, Angels of Abundance and Angels of Loan repayment please bless me with ...................... this or more (write the amount you need to pay) so that I can easily and smoothly pay the loan that I have taken from ................... (write the name of the person or Bank from where you have taken the loan) so that I can happily experience financial freedom now and forever. This or better

Thank you! Thank you! Thank you!

**Note-:** Goddess Abundantia is the goddess of wealth.

Goddess Lakshmi is the goddess of fortune.

Lord Narayan takes care of the Universe.

Goddess Green Tara helps with speed.

Goddess Aeracura takes care of prosperity.

# 27.
# Archangel Prayer for Prosperity

Dear God, Goddess, My Guardian Angel Archangel Michael, please remove all kinds of blockages from my finances.

Archangel Raphael please heal my finances.

Archangel Uriel please bless me with wisdom that will help me to be financially successful and secure.

Archangel Gabriel please help me to communicate with myself and others in such a manner that I grow financially rich every day.

Archangel Chamuel please bring to me positive sources and opportunities of finances, that will make me financially prosperous and rich.

Archangel Zadkiel please help me to forgive anything and anyone including myself, so that I resonate with the vibration of financial abundance.

Archangel Jophiel please beautify my life with financial growth, financial abundance, financial security & financial peace.

Archangel Ariel please bless me with ............ or more (mention the amount) per month. This or better, thank you.

Note-: This prayer will help with business growth, career or anything related to finances

# 28.
# Prayer for Removing Obstacles from Prosperity

Dear Lord Ganesha, you are the remover of obstacles. I request you to remove obstacles from my finances, so that I can experience financial peace, financial growth, financial success and prosperity as soon as possible, now and forever.

Please bless me and my family. This or better, thank you.

**Note -:** Lord Ganesha is the God of wisdom and removes obstacles.

# 29.
# Powerful Prayer for Financial Blessings

Beautiful Divine Goddess Abundantia & Mother Laxmi I surrender to you. Please replace my financial worry with financial peace & freedom.

Shower prosperity, good luck, financial abundance and good fortune from your cornucopia on me, my wallet, bank account and money box.

Bless me with financial abundance so that I enjoy material comforts along with my family.

Guide me in investments so that I earn super profits. Bless me with the gifts of prosperity, good fortune, financial abundance, joy and prosperity.

Thank you for ensuring that I am blessed with financial abundance now and forever. Thank you for

protecting my finances. This or better. Thank you.

**Note-:** Goddess Abundantia is the goddess of wealth.

Goddess Lakshmi is the goddess of fortune

# 30.
# Prayer for Money on Urgent Basis

Dear God, Goddess Aeracura, Goddess Green Tara, Goddess Lakshmi, Saibaba, Swami Samarth, Archangel Ariel & my guardian angels.

I really need _____ (mention the amount that you need) money urgently. Please provide at the earliest. Please make it quick without harming anyone.

I am your child, oh divine realm & you are my source. I have complete faith & trust that you will answer my prayers & bless me with the amount or even more. I surrender to you, please give me strength. This or better. Thank you.

**Note-:** The Gods, Goddesses mentioned help with speed in answering prayers.

# 31.
# Prayer for Selling a Property or Any Object

Dear God, Goddess, Archangel Chamuel, Archangel Ariel, my (owners name) and property's/land/object _____(mention address of the property/land/details of the object) guardian angels I am ready to sell this property/land/object, whoever will benefit from buying this property/land/object give them the wisdom, willingness and finances to purchase this property/land/object so that we both benefit from this deal.

This or better, thank you.

*Note :- Say this prayer every day or at least once a week on Wednesday till property or object is sold. Owner should say this prayer.*

# 32.
# Prayer for Prosperity Consciousness Clearance

"I ask the divine realm to take all the negativity, lower energies, curses, karmas, vows, habits that are stopping me from experiencing financial prosperity to divine light right now & bless me with financial peace, progress, prosperity now and forever."

*Note :- This prayer should be done on a full moon or every day. *

# 33.
# Prayer for Job Interview

Dear God, Goddess, Archangels, Ascended Masters thank you for sending this beautiful opportunity of employment, I am extremely grateful to you.

Please help me to perform intellectually, confidently and courageously in the interview rounds.

Guardian angels of the interview panel and my guardian angels please let the interview panelist be impressed with me and happily give me the best job offer soon.

Please bless me with this wonderful employment opportunity, this or better.

Thank you Thank you Thank you

# 34.
# Prayer for Finding Job

Dear God, Goddess Archangels, please help me to find a corporate job in which I will be extremely happy, successful. Let this job be in a prosperous firm.

Please bless me with a package of _____ or more per annum and a bonus of _____ per year.

Please let me have a good work life balance.

Please let me experience _____ (mention all that you want in the organization)

Please bless me with Good boss, colleagues and people to work with. Please let me experience success and progress in my career. This or better thank you.

# 35.
# Prayer for Self - Acceptance

Dear God, Goddess, Archangel Chamuel please help me to love and accept myself truly and unconditionally.

This or better.

Thank you! Thank you! Thank you!

# 36.
# Prayer for Self-Confidence

Dear Divine and Angels please help me to love myself truly and unconditionally. Please make me realize, accept and appreciate my true potential.

Please heal my anxiety, emotions, any past life trauma and all that which is blocking me from being self-confident.

I request you with all my being to increase my self-confidence, self-esteem and self-respect, so that I shine in divine light and illuminate my life and that of people around me.

Help me Divine and my whole spiritual team of Angels and spirit guides to believe in myself and you, also help me to take positive steps to increase my confidence and self -love. This or better, thank you.

*Note :- Apart from the above prayer chant " Divine Shine" continuously when you need that extra confidence for an interview presentation etc.*

# 37.
# Prayer to Stop People from Spoiling Reputation

Dear God, Goddess, Archangel Michael please protect my reputation and promote my goodwill.

It's my will to be at peace and enjoy a good reputation.

I request you to please release all slander, gossip about me, my work, my family to divine light.

Please help me & my family to think, act and conduct ourselves in such a manner that we earn good reputation and goodwill.

Bless everyone with divine love and wisdom, this or better. Thank you!

# 38.
# Prayer for Joy

Dear God, Goddess, Archangel Jophiel and Ascended Masters please beautify my thoughts in such a manner that my mind, body and soul is full of joy, peace, hope and vibrance

Please beautify my home, workplace and surroundings with positive energy so that it boosts my morale and encourages me to be extremely blissful and at peace.

This or better.

 Thank you. Thank you!

# 39.
# Prayers for Time Management

Dear God, Goddess and Archangel Metatron, I really need your help to manage time easily and do all important task in priority without any procrastination.

Please help me to plan my day and life efficiently. Please help me to prioritize and manage time most effectively to attain my life purpose easily and smoothly. This or better thank you.

# 40.
# Prayer for Life Purpose

Dear God, Goddess, Archangel Chamuel and Archangel Michael, please help me to clearly understand my life purpose easily and quickly.

Please give me the courage to follow my life's purpose easily and happily. Please bless me with the support that I need to carry on my life purpose. I also request you to help me manage time, myself and others in an effective manner to be able to do justice to my life purpose.

Please let my life purpose support me in every possible way.

This or better, thank you.

# 41.
# Prayer for Divine Grace during Tough Times

Dear God, you know what I am going through. I hand over my struggles, stress, grief, and disappointment to you.

I have complete faith that you and your army of angels are here with me for my aid. Hold me and calm me down, bless me with strength and faith.

Cradle me in your arms and envelope me in peace. Equip me with knowingness, that you are taking care of everything.

Please heal & fill me with hope, faith and positivity so that I can be a magnet of divine magnanimity.

Please illuminate my mind, body, and soul with your divine light. Let me experience divine intervention and miracles. Please, God, be with me in every moment now and forever.

# 42.
# Prayer for Increasing Faith in Divine

Dear God, Goddess, Archangel Chamuel & my guardian angels please help me to strengthen my faith in the divine.

Archangel Jophiel beautify my thoughts when I am feeling low.

Archangel Uriel with your Divine light brighten my faith in the divine.

Archangel Michael cut all the cords of negativity, lower energies and psychic attacks that are draining my faith in the divine.

Archangel Chamuel please help me to receive & give love to the divine unconditionally.

Dear almighty, thank you for helping me to experience divine miracles now and forever. This or better. Thank You.

# 43.
# Prayer to 9 Forms of Goddess Durga

Supreme Powerful Goddess Durga, my divine mother, you descend in your warrior form in these 9 days to destroy evil and restore light.

I welcome you, your 9 powerful manifestations into my life and request you to peacefully remove all forms of negativity from my and my family's life and our whole being. I seek blessings from your 9 forms Maa.

Goddess Shailaputri please bless me with strength.

Goddess Brahmachrini bless me with strong will power.

Goddess Chandraghanta please bless me with peace, and prosperity & strengthen my aura.

Goddess Kushmanda bless me with creativity & good health.

Goddess Skandamata bless me with divine wisdom.

Goddess Kathyayini bless me with a happy and harmonious relationship.

Goddess Kalratri please me with your divine protection.

Goddess Mahagauri please purify my soul & wash away my sins.

Goddess Siddhidhatri please bless me with siddhis and protect me in all directions of time.

I bow with love and respect to you my Divine Mother Goddess Durga and all your 9 forms.

This or better. Thank you

Om Doom Durgaya Namaha

*Note Say Prayer at any time once every day in Navratri*

You can also say this prayer every day or once a week.

# 44.
# Prayer to Seek Miracles

Dear God, Goddess and Archangels Hamied, please develop an attitude of wonder and gratitude in me. Please bless me with the perspective of seeing good in all things in a wise manner.

I really wish to see and experience miracles. I am ready to receive infinite miracles in my life with your grace. Please bless me with miracles today and let me experience them now and forever, this or better, thank you.

# 45.
## Prayer to Show God's Presence

Dear God, Goddess and Angels, I really wish to see and feel you. I wish to communicate with you clearly and understand your guidance, and signs so please show me your presence in a way that I can clearly understand and see.

# 46.
# Prayer for Conception

Dear God, Goddess, and Mother Mary my and my husband's/ wife guardian angels and the guardian angels of our child / children in heaven I and my husband wish from the bottom of our heart to become parents of our biological child/children.

We request you to grace us with the joy of parenthood so that we can share the love in our hearts with our children.

Please heal our body, mind and soul, so that we can conceive our biological child or children easily and soon. We release all the karmas, curses, mental and physical blockages to Divine light. Please send a beautiful soul as our child/children who will bring a lot of happiness, pride and love into our life.

Please bless us with a healthy baby who will grow beautifully, perfectly and will have a long, healthy happy life and who will truly love us.

We have complete faith and trust that you will bless us with the joy of parenthood soon.

This is better, thank you.

# 47.
# Prayer for Safe Pregnancy

Dear God, Goddess, Archangels, Saibaba, Kuldevi or Kuldev (family deity), Swami Samarth & Saint Jude, thank you for blessing me with this divine child. Please bless this child with a happy, healthy, long, successful, loving life and let my pregnancy ahead be healthy, safe and smooth.

Let my baby grow in a beautiful, healthy and happy manner. This or better thank you.

Note-: Prayers 45,46,47 to be done along with proper prenatal, and post-natal care, and doctors consultation.

# 48
# Prayer for Easy Delivery of Child

Dear God, Goddess, Archangels my, my partners and my child's guardian angels, thank you for blessing us with this beautiful baby in my womb.

Please let the child grow beautiful, perfectly, and healthy.

I am looking forward to the day of delivery of our precious child. I surrender all my fears to divine light & request you to bless me, our family & our baby with emotional & physical strength.

Goddess Ambe Maa, Goddess Dana, Mother Mary, Goddess Kuan Yin, Archangel Raphael I prefer to have natural delivery, however I surrender to you the mode of delivery as I have complete faith that you will choose the mode that is for my and our child's highest good and safety.

Please be present at the time of delivery of my child & guide the doctors, nurses, me & the child in such a way that the delivery of my child is smooth, easy, safe, quick & as painless as possible. This or better, thank you.

# 49.
# Removing Obstacles or Wish Fulfillment Prayer

Dear Divine it is my will to……………………………….. (mention wish) I request you to please remove all the obstacles and create big happy miracles in my ……………. (mention situations e.g. Conception, health, Love life, finances, Career, Child's education, Selling or buying property, promotion.)

Please counsel and guide me so that I am emotionally ready to experience progress in my…………………….. (mention the same situation as above). Please send the right assistance and helpful people who will help me achieve my wish.

Please help me to take actions that will make my dream a reality. This or better. Thank you.

*Note :- Every day after saying the above prayer. Chant :- Om Gam Ganapataye Namaha 108 times.

The above step is optional.*

# 50.
# Lord Ganesha Prayer for Removing Obstacles

Dear Lord Ganesha, you are the son of mighty Lord Shiva and Goddess Parvati.

You are the remover of all obstacles & God of new beginnings, intellect & wisdom.

Divine Lord Ganesha, you with Goddess Saraswati bless me with divine wisdom & along with Goddess Lakshmi please me with good fortune and prosperity.

Please remove all obstacles from my....................(e.g. fiancés, love life etc.) and bless me with ........................... (state your wish)

This or better, thank you!

Note-: Goddess Saraswati is the Goddess of knowledge and wisdom.

# 51.
# Saint Jude Prayer for Wish Fulfilment

Dear God, Goddess and Saint Jude, I call upon you earnestly to help me & stay with me in the time of my need.

Saint Jude you are the patron of hopeless cases and things almost despaired for, so please grace me with the blessings of granting my wish .................... (mention your wish, be specific)

I have complete faith & trust in your power of bringing miracles in my life . I thank you and I promise that once my wish is granted, I will donate ............. (mention the amount) and will publish that you blessed me with the miracle I asked for.

Thank you!

**Note :- Prayer has to be said for 9 days, anytime is ok. If you miss a day, restart.

Once a wish is granted you can publish "thank you Saint Jude" by keeping your WhatsApp or fb status. Donations can be made to anyone who is needy or NGOs.

# 52.
# Prayer for Healing Relationship

Dear God, Goddess, Angles of Peace my guardian angels and my partner's guardian angels (can say partners name or anyone with whom peace and harmony is required)

Please heal our relationship, beautify our thoughts towards each other. Guide us to take necessary steps to heal our relationship. Make our relationship stronger. Let the love that we feel towards each other increase every day.

Let us treat each other with respect & help us to stay loyal towards each other. Please let there be love, harmony, peace, happiness, trust between us forever.

Thank you God, Goddess, Angles of Peace, Guardian Angels.

# 53.
# Resolution of Conflict Prayer

Dear God, Goddess, Archangel Raguel, my guardian angels and guardian angels of ................ (name of the persons with whom conflict is there) I am ready to be at peace.

I request you to heal all issues that are causing conflict between me and .............. (Name of the person with whom conflict is there).

Please replace every negativity between us with divine positivity and light. Please help us to be in harmony with each other. Please intervene and resolve all misunderstandings, negative karma, hurt, disappointment in such a way that there is peace and light in our mind and souls.

Please bless us with divine wisdom so that we radiate in the true nature of our soul which is of pure love. Please send millions of peace angels to bring peace and harmony in my and .................... (person with whom conflict is there) interaction. Please resolve this conflict soon and in a manner that is comfortable and results in a win-win situation for everyone involved. This or better. Thank you.

Note-: This prayer can be said for any kind of conflict with anyone.

# 54.
# Prayer for a Soul Crossing Over

Dear God, Goddess, Archangel Azrael and the guardian angels of ................ (person who has passed away) please help the soul to transit peacefully and easily.

Please send millions of angels to heal and comfort the soul and the loved ones in this time of transition.

Please bless the soul and convey our love.

This or better. Thank you.

# 55.
# Prayers for Ancestral Healing

"Dear Divine, please bless me, my family & my ancestors. Please heal our entire lineage and ancestors from all kind of trauma, negativity, karmas. Please forgive us and our ancestors for all kinds of sins that we have committed knowingly, unknowingly, intentionally or unintentionally. This or better, thank you."

Note :- Say this prayer on Monday or whenever your tradition pays homage to ancestor e.g., sarva pitru Amavasya in Hindus

# 56.
# Prayer for World Peace & Well Being

Dear God, Goddess, Archangels, millions of peace angels & humanitarian angels, please remove from our mother earth and its inhabitants all kinds of negativity, lower energies, psychic attacks, epidemics, pandemics, economic - social crisis. Please send this to divine light and replace it with emotional and physical well-being, progressing economy, good health, security, peace & harmony.

Mother Kuan yin, Archangel Raguel, Archangel Uriel & Archangel Zadkiel please infuse love, compassion and forgiveness in the hearts, minds and souls of every living being on earth. Please shower divine wisdom on every being on Mother Earth.

Please envelope the earth and all its living beings with unconditional love & peace. This or better.

**Note :-** Prayer is for sending healing energies to the world and us from viruses, wars, economic and social crisis.

Goddess Kuan Yin is the Goddess of mercy and compassion.

Archangel Zadkiel helps with forgiveness.

# 57.
# Prayer for Country

I call upon the divine God, Goddess, Archangels,

Guardian Angels of ………. (Country name) and Guardian Angels of every ……….. (citizen/resident) to bless our beautiful country with peace, prosperity, protection and development.

Please bless our country with a good environment.

Infuse divine wisdom in each and every resident of ………… (Country name) so that peace and harmony prevails.

Please cover ………….. (Country name) with a divine shield of protection and healing so that our country and its residents are safe in all directions of time.

This or better, thank you

Please read the prayer at least once today.

# 58.
# Prayer for Soldier

Dear God, Goddess, Archangels thank you for blessing us with these selfless soldiers who protect all of us day and night.

Please protect them and give them and their family the strength to carry on with their noble purpose.

Please shower them and their families with good health, love, happiness and prosperity.

Please envelope them in your purple shield and safeguard them from all kinds of dangers so that they can easily and happily serve our nation with pride.

This or better, thank you.

# 59.
# Prayer for Child's Academic Success

Dear God, Goddess, Lord Ganesha, Goddess Saraswati, my child's guardian angels he/she is appearing for ............ (mention exam name) please help him/her to prepare successfully for the exams.

Lord Ganesha and Archangel Michael please remove all obstacles, and distractions that are creating hindrances in my child's academic success to divine light.

Please equip my child with resources that are important for his/ her academic success.

Archangel Zadkiel help him/her to remember and recall all the information that is required for cleaning the exam successfully.

Archangel Uriel please help my child to be confident and calm while writing the exams. It is my will and my child's will to clear the exams successfully with ........ (mention marks) or better marks / grade / percentage please grant our will. This or better, thank you.

*Note :- Prayer for academic success to be read by parents or teacher or guardian*

Lord Ganesha and Goddess Saraswati blesses with wisdom.

Archangel Zadkiel helps with retaining information.

Action has to be taken by the student by studying.

# 60.
# Prayer for Academic Success

Dear God, Goddess, Lord Ganesha, Goddess Saraswati, my guardian angels, I am appearing for _____ (mention exam name) please help me to prepare successfully for the exams.

Lord Ganesha and Archangel Michael please remove all obstacles, distractions that are creating hindrance in my academic success to divine light.

Please equip me with resources that are important for my academic success.

Archangel Zadkiel help me to remember and recall all the information that is required for clearing the exam successfully.

Archangel Uriel please help me to be confident and calm while writing the exams.

It is my will to clear the exams successfully with …………..(mention marks) or better marks/grade/percentage please grant my will. This or better, thank you.

*Note :- This prayer needs to be said by one appearing for the exams.*

Lord Ganesha and Goddess Saraswati blesses with wisdom.

Archangel Zadkiel helps with retaining information.

Action has to be taken by the student by studying

# 61.
# Prayer for Adequate Rain and To Stop Excess Rain

Dear God, Goddess, Archangels thank you for the rains that you blessed us with today. Please continue to bless us with adequate rain, so that we have enough water.

We request you to bless with rains, those places on earth that are barren, dry and have less water supply.

Let our earth always receive adequate rains so that there is greenery, safety and happiness all around.

This or better, thank you.

# 62.
# Prayer If You Are Experiencing Natural Calamity

Dear God, Goddess Archangels, Mother Earth we are facing _____ (mention the calamity like cyclone, earthquake) in _____ (mention location). Please stop this ____ (mention type of calamity) and envelope it with divine light for healing and transmutation. Please calm and heal Mother Earth and everyone affected by this calamity.

Please give our frontline workers strength to handle themselves and everyone. Please help the rescue staff to rescue people and animals safely. Please guide the authorities to take and execute decisions that will benefit everyone. Please let the departed souls transition peacefully to divine light

Please rehabilitate people and restore all material aspects, infrastructure. Please let all losses be recovered and replaced with prosperity. Please give emotional and physical strength to everyone especially the ones who have lost their loved ones.

Please keep everyone safe and protected. This or better thank you.

# 63.
# Prayer for Protection from Natural Calamities like Cyclone, Tsunami, Earthquake

Dear God, Goddess Archangels and Mother we have come to know that there is a possibility of _____ (mention natural calamity like cyclone or earthquake).

Please let this natural calamity be avoided by your divine powers.

Please calm Mother Earth and heal her with divine light. Please protect Mother Earth and us. Please keep us safe in all directions of time from all kinds of harm.

We seek forgiveness for all the times we knowingly or unknowingly hurt Mother earth or her inhabitants. This or better thank you.

# 64.
# Prayer for Raising Children

Dear God, Goddess and Archangels thank you for blessing me with these child / children. Lately it has been challenging for me to handle ........................ (child's name). I really need your support & guidance to handle this gift of yours. Please bless us with wisdom, support and patience to be good parents.

I request you to bless........................... (Child's name) with wisdom so that they are able to follow the right path. Please bless them with patience, good friends and people so that they are able to navigate easily in life and receive proper guidance. Please remove their addictions from ............................... (E.g. Phone, Alcohol) so that they are able to focus on achieving academic, career & life goals.

Archangel Raguel and Goddess Kuan Yin please resolve the conflict between............................ (child's name) and us so that there is peace, love and harmony at home. Please bless them with emotional strength, ambition and ability to work hard & smart so that they can achieve their life purpose and career goals.

# 65.
# Prayer for Safety and Guidance of Children

Dear God, Goddess, Archangels my guardian angels, my husband's (or wife) guardian angels and guardian angels of our children, thank you for blessing us with the joy of parenthood.

We are so grateful and happy for this gift from the divine realm.

Please be with us in this journey, guide us at every step and help us to follow your guidance so that our children are happy, healthy and safe.

Angels of joy, healing and growth please heal our children and help our children to grow emotionally, physically, intellectually and spiritually in a happy, safe and comfortable manner.

Please bless us and our children with emotional and intellectual wisdom.

Please protect us and our children from all kinds of negativity, lower energies, dangers, entities and curses. Please guide us with the right food, beverages that will nurture and nourish our children.

Please send the right people who will help us and our children in this journey of life.

Please envelope us and our children in divine wisdom, love and protection now and forever. I request you God, Goddess, Archangels to bless our children with a happy, healthy, long, loving and successful life. This or better. Thank you.

# 66.
# Angel Magick Spell for Finding Lost Item

If you have lost something take any piece of clean cloth of any size & while tying a knot say the prayer.

"Dear God Goddess Archangel Chamuel I have lost ……. (mention the thing you lost) Please help me to find it, thank you"

Once you find the lost item untie the knot and give gratitude.

This simple spell always works, in case if you do not find the lost item despite doing this spell then understand that the thing has gone out of your life for good.

# 67.
# Prayer to Find a Missing Person/Pet

Dear God, Goddess, Archangel Chamuel, Saint Anthony _____ (mention person/pet's name) is missing.

I, their family, friends are really worried about them. Please protect them. Keep them safe. Please give them and us emotional strength.

Please give them guidance and support to contact us and get support. Please send them the right people that will help and protect them.

Please help us to find them soon. Please guide the authorities, rescue team to find them asap.

Please help us in this time of need. This or better.

# 68.
# Prayer for Positive Thoughts

Dear God & Archangel Jophiel please beautify my thoughts & help me to mould my thoughts, beliefs & actions in such a manner that I feel positive, peaceful & happy. This or better. Thank you.

# 69.
# Prayer for Abundance

Dear God Narayan, Goddess Lakshmi, Goddess Abundantia, Lord Ganesha and Kuber, Archangel Ariel, Archangel Zadkiel and millions of Angels of Abundance, please shower infinite amount of financial prosperity on me. This or better. Thank you.

# 70.
# Prayer during Tough Times

Dear God please fill my heart with immense faith and trust in you and Angels so that I am continuously blessed with peace, security & wisdom.

# 71.
# Short Prayers for Hair, Skin and Weight

Hair :- Dear God, Goddess, Archangel Jophiel and Archangel Raphael make my hair healthy, long, beautiful, voluminous, silky, naturally black (mention color) and strong. Please heal my scalp and hair and support each strand of hair with love.

Skin :- Dear God, Goddess, Archangel Jophiel & Archangel Raphael Please heal & beautify my skin so that each and every pore of my skin glows with God's and Goddess's divine light.

Thank you God, Goddess, Archangel Jophiel & Raphael for making my skin so gorgeous, young, extremely radiant, clear, beautiful and glowing.

Weight :- Dear God, Goddess, Archangel Raphael please make my metabolism active in such a manner that my body maintains its ideal weight. Please bless me with an hourglass figure (for women) or V shaped body (for men). Thank You.

# 72.
# Prayer for New Year

Dear Divine, please help me to realise my potential and guide me to use it for my highest good. Please help me to be a better person and bless me and my family with Divine Health, Divine Joy, Divine Love, Divine Abundance & Divine wisdom

Please let this year be one of the best years of my life. Let this year be full of pleasant memories

this or better. Thank you.

# 73.
# Short Prayers to Call upon Archangel Chamuel for Love

Archangel Chamuel is the angel of love, if your love needs some help then call upon Archangel Chamuel.

**Prayer for Healing :-**

The most important thing is to heal ones heart, say the following prayer "Dear Divine Archangel Chamuel and Archangel Raphael heal my heart and fill it

with divine light and wisdom, this or better, thank you."

**Prayer for Identifying the blockages:-**

Before going to bed, write on a piece of paper "Dear God please help me to identify the blockages in my dream and also guide me to heal it, help me remember the dream when I wake up."

**Prayer for Breaking the old patterns:-**

"Dear God, Goddess, Archangel Michael, please clear any blockages and old patterns that are stopping me from experiencing a happy, successful, loving, committed love life. This or better, thank you."

**Prayer for Self-Love:-**

"Dear Divine and Archangel Chamuel help me to love myself truly and unconditionally, this or better, thank you."

**Prayer for Calling on your life partner:-**

"Dear Divine, my romantic partner's guardian angel and my guardian angel, I request you to help us to meet each other and also to communicate with each other so that we can have a happy successful loving marriage now and forever, this or better, thank you."

# 74.
# Prayer for Everyday

Dear God bless me with so much positivity so that I am always happy and at peace.

Please help me to smile and laugh every day wholeheartedly.

Let peace and happiness

be present in every moment

This or better thank you.

# 75.
## Prayer to Make New Friends

Dear God, Goddess, Archangel Chamuel I feel lonely on this beautiful earth and miss having genuine true friends.

I request you to please bless me with friends who will see the good in me and motivate me to be better.

Please bless me with trustworthy friends who will see & understand with compassion what's broken in me and help me to heal it with their unconditional love and friendship.

Please bless me with friends with whom my soul grows with happiness, joy, wisdom and laughter.

This or better, Thank you.

# 76.
# Prayer for Happy Holidays

Dear God, Goddess, Archangel Raphael and Archangel Michael thank you for blessing us with this wonderful vacation.

We really needed this break, please let us have lots of good memories and positive fun on this holiday.

Please keep us safe and protected all the time.

Let this vacation be one of the best vacations of our lives, this or better. Thank you.

# 77.
# Prayer for Tarot Readers

I with the grace of almighty invoke the Divine Gods, Goddesses, Archangels, Tarot Angels to increase my intuition, accurate understanding & interpretation of the Tarot Cards and my psychic powers.

I humbly request you all to build & raise my confidence, trust and faith in Divine and myself.

Please cleanse my Tarot cards and space where I do tarot readings and infuse it with Divine wisdom and grace.

Please clearly guide me throughout the session so that I am able to clearly interpret the tarot cards and provide accurate guidance for the highest good of the querent.

This or better, thank you.

# 78.
# Prayer for Cleansing Your Home with Archangel Michael

I call upon Divine God, Goddess, Archangel Michael and the power angels to cleanse each and every part of my home with divine energies.

This or better thank you.

# 79.
# Prayer for a New Home

Dear God, Goddess, Archangels, we really wish to stay in a beautiful house. It is my and my family's will to be in a happy and a spacious positive home.

We release all blockages that are stopping us from enjoying the bliss of staying in a beautiful, spacious home of our own to divine light.

We surrender to you and ask you to bless us with a home in which I and my family will be extremely happy.

A home in which we will prosper and enjoy a harmonious, loving bond with each other. This or better thank you.

*Note :- Say the prayer once a day, any time alone or with family.*

# 80.
# Prayer for Finding a Good Maid

Dear God, Goddess, Archangel Chamuel, I am ready to delegate work at my place, please send an extremely good maid who will work diligently and honestly at the price that I have decided in terms of remuneration. Please let her be trustworthy.

Please let this maid be hygienic and have a good attitude. Please ensure that my family and I will have a cordial professional relationship with this maid.

Please let this maid work for us for a long time in a way that is professionally beneficial for both of us.

This or better, thank you.

*Note :- If you want a driver, nanny or caretaker replace the word maid in the above prayer with driver or caretaker.*

# 81.
# Prayer for Finding Employee

Dear God, Goddess, Archangel Chamuel, I am looking for (staff position) for (organisation name). I am sure that there is a capable candidate who is also desperately looking for this employment opportunity.

I request you to help me get in touch with this candidate who will work diligently & honestly at the remuneration that (organisation name) has decided which is also beneficial to the candidate.

Please ensure that post employment this candidate who will become an employee shares a cordial professional relationship organisation. Please let them play a very important positive role in making the organisation grow.

Please also ensure that this employee works for the organisation for a long time in a way that is professionally beneficial for both the employee and the organisation. This or better thank you.

# 82.
# Prayer for Decision Making

Dear God, Goddess and Archangels I am confused regarding _____ (mention the situation for which you need to make a decision). I need clarity to make a decision regarding this situation.

I request you to please give me clarity and guidance to take the right decision that will be for my highest good and that will bring joy, love, happiness and abundance.

Please help me to clearly understand and follow your guidance happily and smoothly. This or better. Thank you.

# Frequently Asked Questions (FAQs)

1. How many times do I need to say the prayers?
   - Once a day is enough
2. How long should I say the prayer?
   - It depends till what time you would want the blessing e.g. we need money forever or emotional wisdom always so you have to say it every day however if you want to have a child then pregnancy prayer you will recite till you become pregnant.
3. How much time does it take for a prayer to get answered?
   - At times it gets answered instantly or it takes years or it's answered in a completely different manner e.g. A person may be praying for a new job but divine feels she should be doing a business hence she will get a lot of business ideas or opportunities.

4. What do I need to do so that my prayers get answered soon?

   A. Let go -: We have all heard the more you run behind something the further it goes away from you so pray without expectations.

   B. Faith-: You need to have unshakeable or strong faith in the divine and believe that the divine will surely answer your prayer in a way that is for your highest good.

   C. Action-: You need to take action to ensure that your prayer gets answered e.g. if a person is doing the academic prayer but is not studying or if a person is doing the fitness prayer and not eating healthy or exercising then the prayer will not get answered.

   D. Karma-: One has to be mindful of their karmas.

5. Can I pray for others?

   - Yes, you can by taking the individual's name in the prayer e.g. If the statement is "Please bless me" you will say "Please bless X"

6. Any specific time to do prayers?

   - Whenever you get time.

7. Can I do prayers while travelling?

   - Yes

8. Can I do prayers during menstruation?

- It's up to you. I personally feel prayers is a way to connect with the divine and menstruation is given by the divine

9. Do I have to say prayers every day?

    - When you pray you are creating energy hence regular prayers create a positive energy build-up. So it helps if you pray every day.

10. There are so many prayers, which ones should I say?

    - The ones that are a priority for you e.g. if your priority is to get a job or improvement in finances then say the finance prayer.

11. Anything I need to keep in mind while doing the prayers?

    - Do it with faith and not fear.

12. Can I do prayers before the bath?

    - If you had a bath once a day after that, anytime is the best.

13. Can I do the prayers before going to bed?

    - Yes.

14. I feel bored doing the prayers or don't get the time?

    - If you have been doing prayers regularly your ego will feel powerless and may trick you by making you feel bored or making you feel you don't have time so make peace with it and do the prayers.

15. Can there be any negative effects of the prayers?

    - No there should not be as you are praying to the divine and the divine is ever-loving however prayers are not meant to replace any doctor's advice or professional advice or medicines. You also have to take proper precautions and safety measures.

www.ingramcontent.com/pod-product-compliance
Lightning Source LLC
LaVergne TN
LVHW061555070526
838199LV00077B/7056